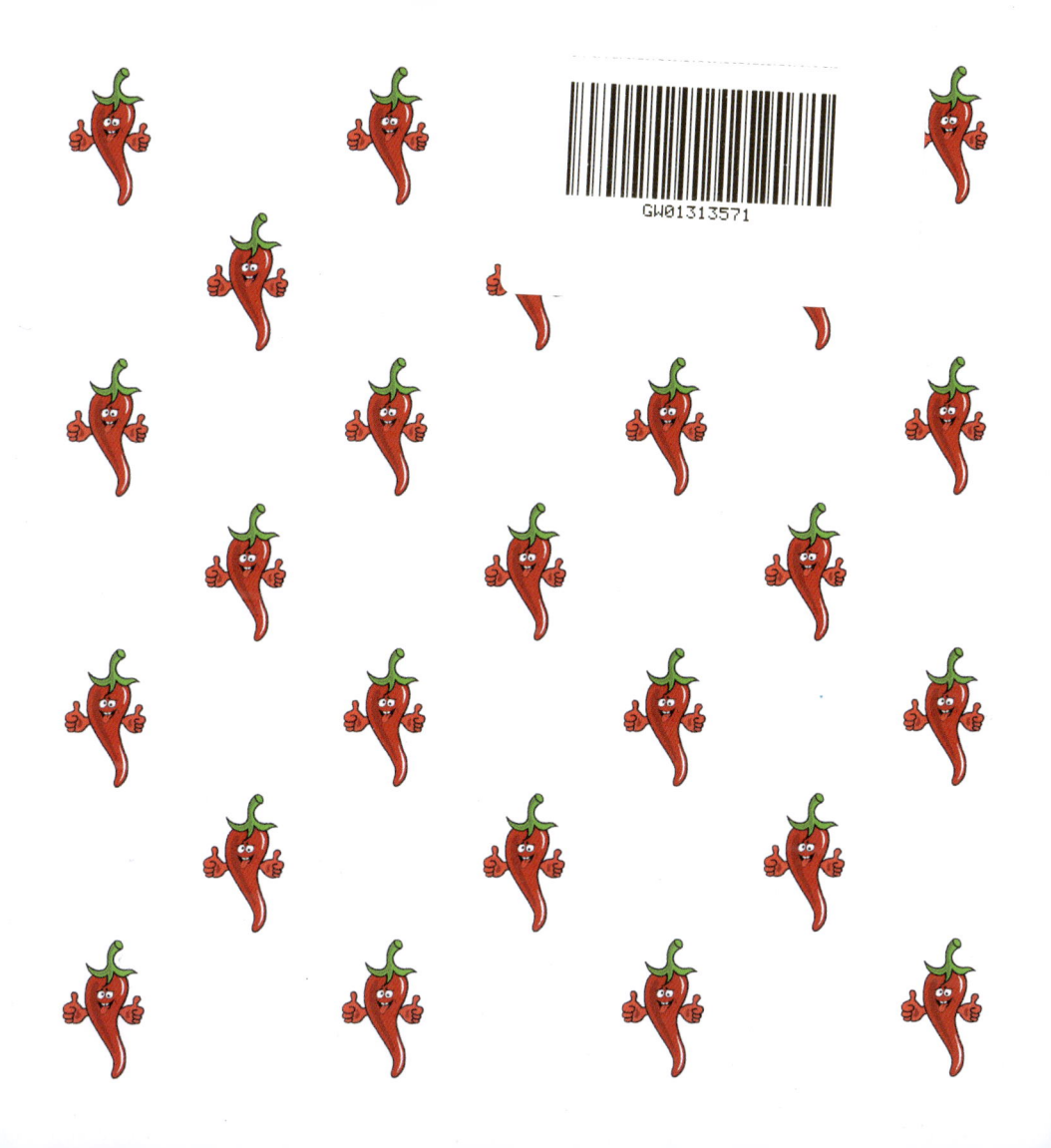

THE YUMS

Chilli is a little bit naughty

he is always being told
to stand still

He likes running around
like a loony

and only stops
when he feels quite ill

Chilli also likes
bouncing and jumping

He tries to get
really high

He once jumped
off a shelf

and landed in some
shepherds pie!

He swam through the mash
to safety

and dived off
the edge of the dish

He landed
in a pot of chutney

and ended up
covered in squish!

Chilli plans to play
hide and seek

when Mum tries
to find him tonight

He is going to hide
behind Leek

then jump out
and give Mum a fright

He once hid from Mum
using camouflage

and lay down in front of
the ketchup

Mum tried to find him
for ages and ages

but after an hour
she gave up

Chilli is forgiven
for being so naughty

because he makes
people warm inside

He should have been here
to say 'Goodbye'

but he's just run away
to hide

(Come back Chilli!)

Created by Mary Ingram

Read about Chilli's friends ...

www.theyums.co.uk

Potato

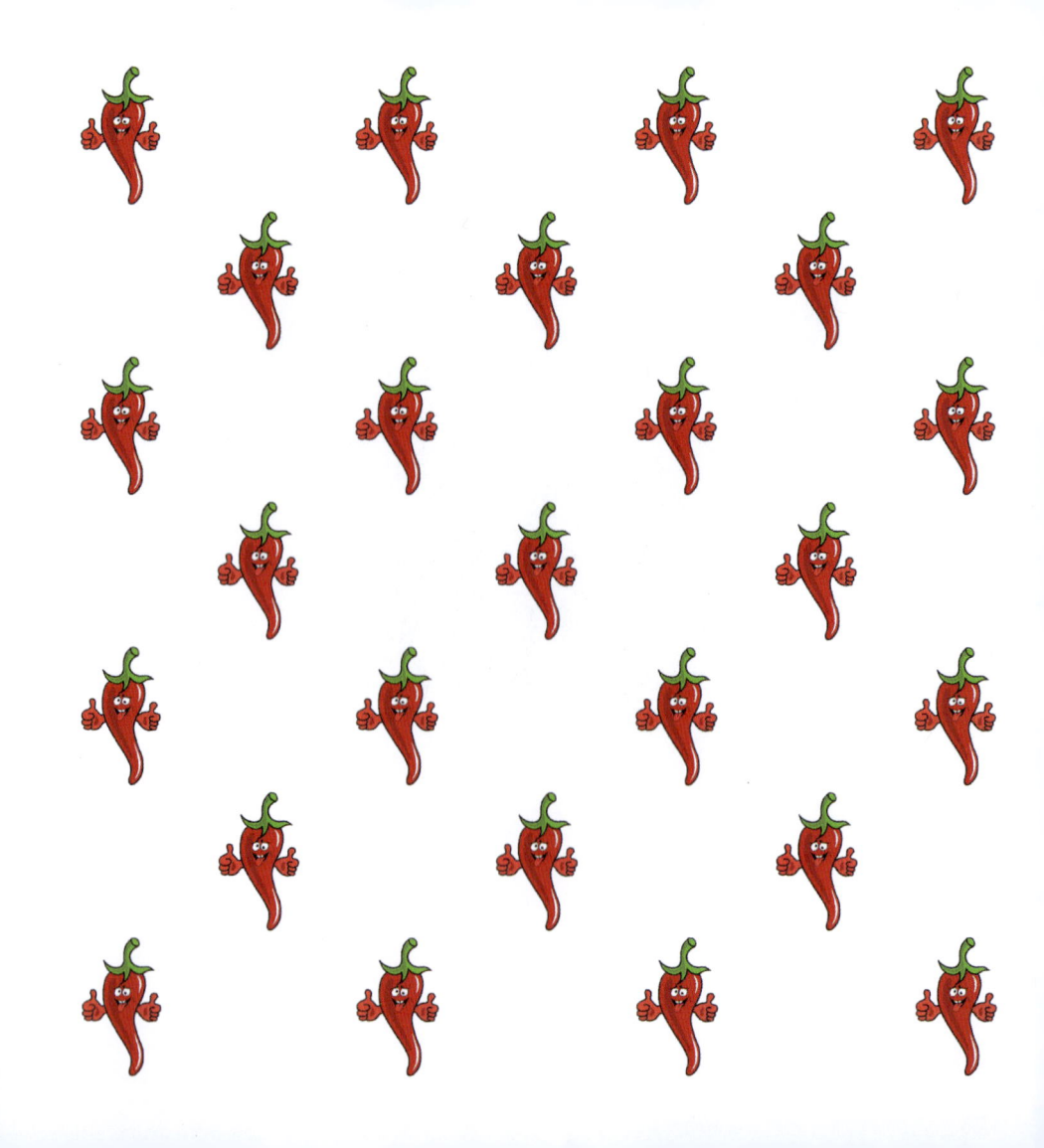

Printed in Great Britain
by Amazon